About The Author and Illustrator

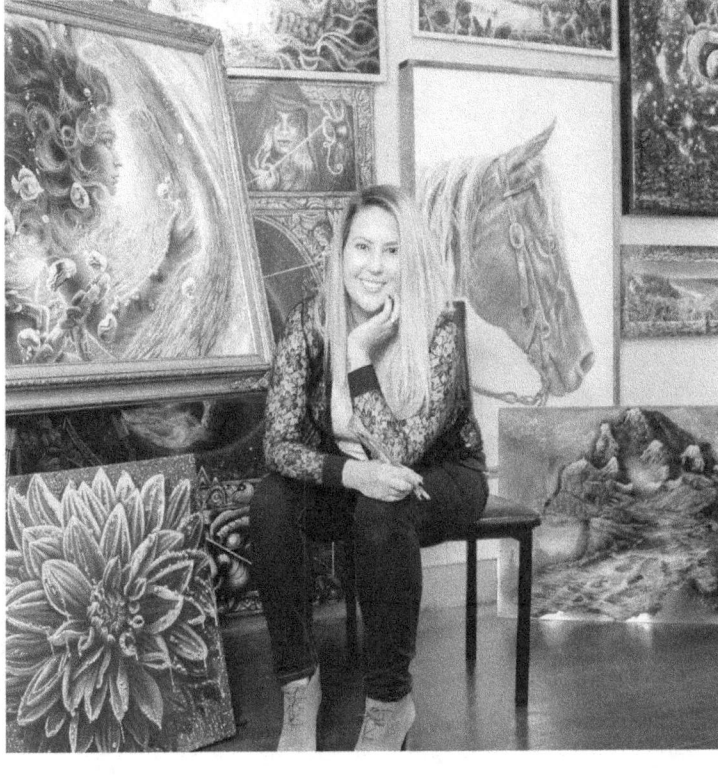

Dakota Daetwiler was born and raised in Humboldt County, CA. She was always really into art, and loved to draw when she was a child. Dakota remembers fondly her vivid imagination as a kid, she would daydream and visualize a world of magic and wonder. She likes to ioncorporate that sense of wonder into her books and paintings today.

Dakota's main message is always the same, no matter if you're viewing her paintings, books, sculptures or illustrations: "Life is magical."

"Thank you for purchasing this book. If you would like to view any of my other works or paintings please visit my website below."

-Dakota Daetwiler

www.PaintingsByDakota.com

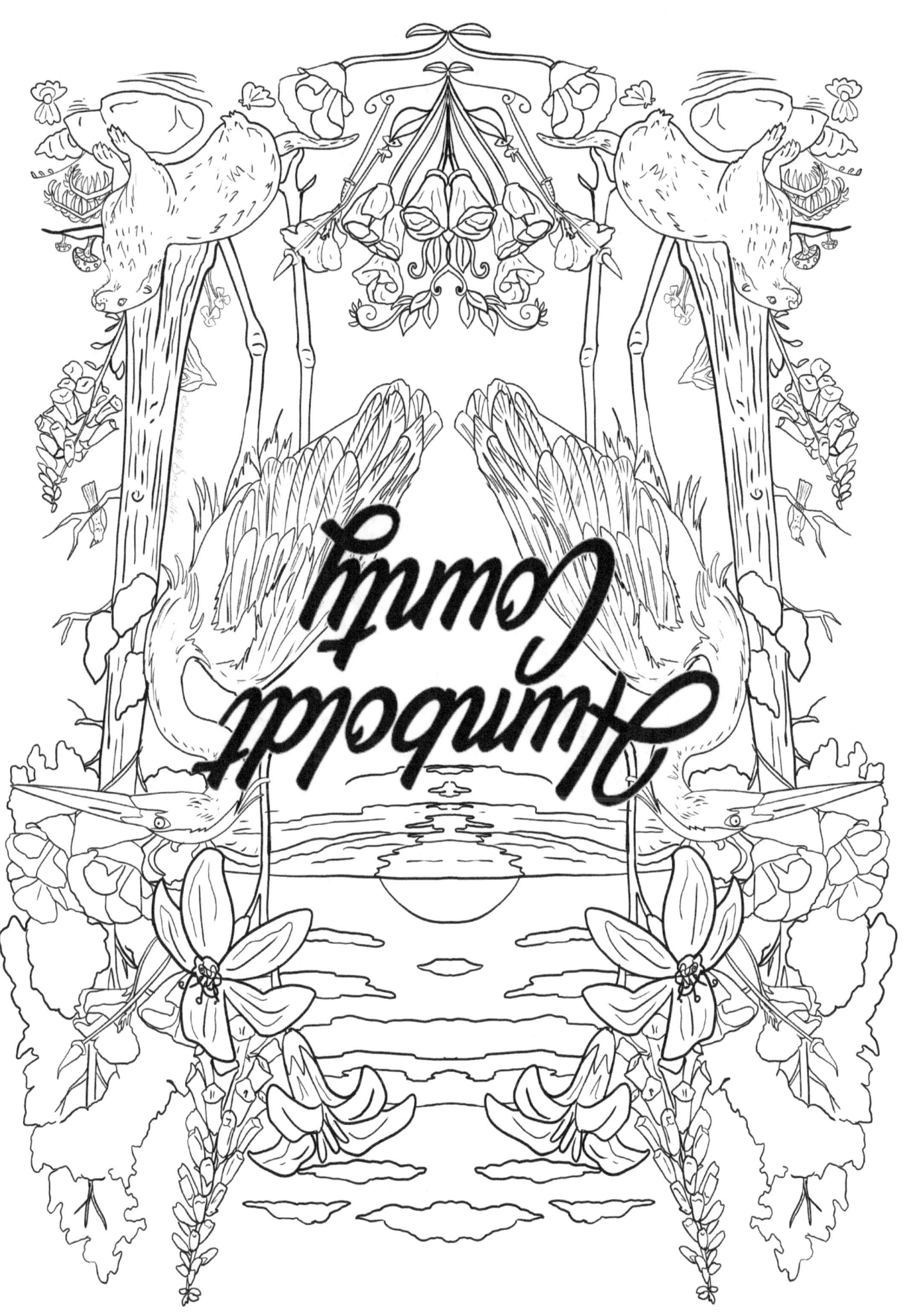
Humboldt County

Draw your favorite animal

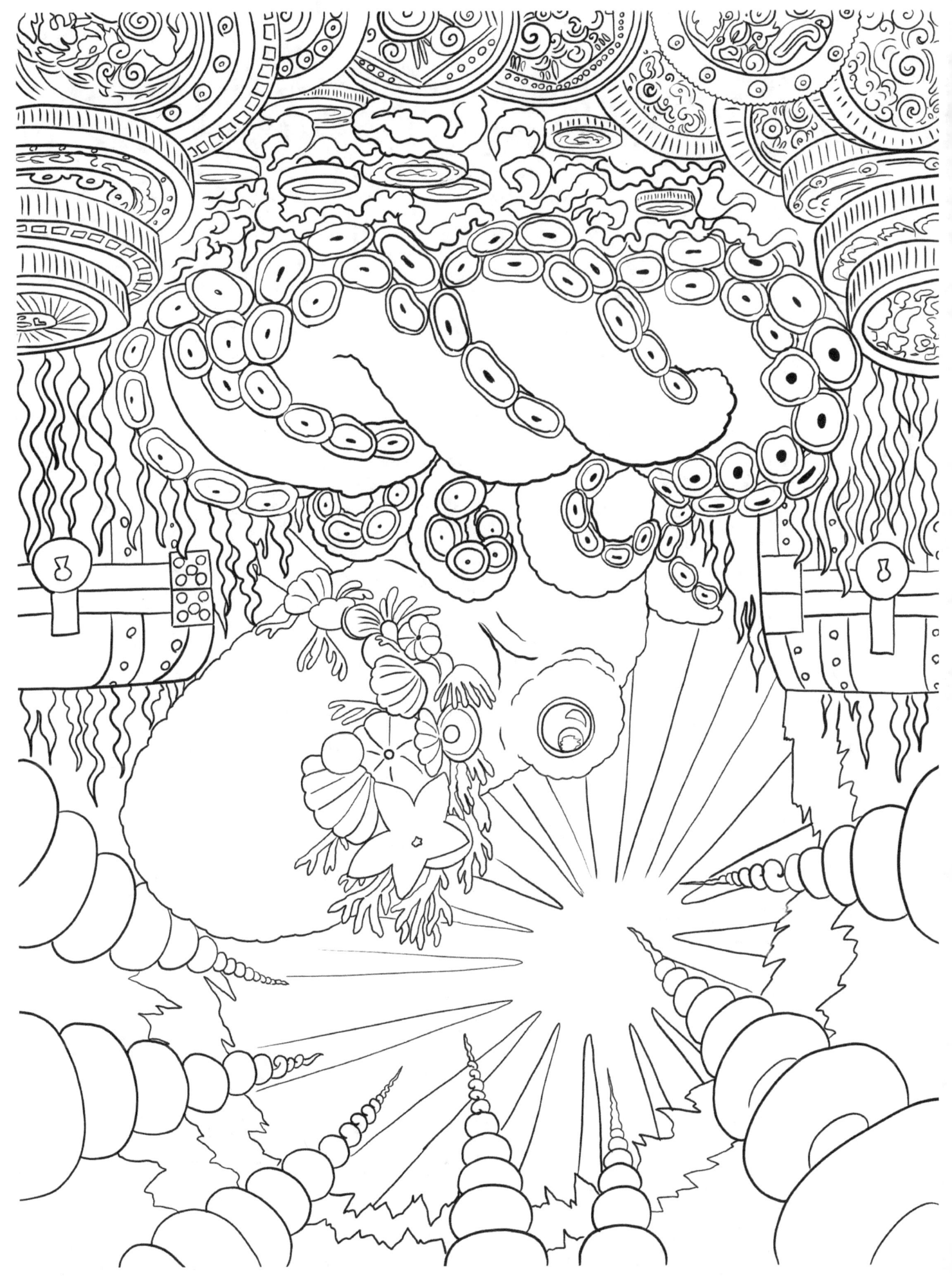

Draw your favorite local scenery

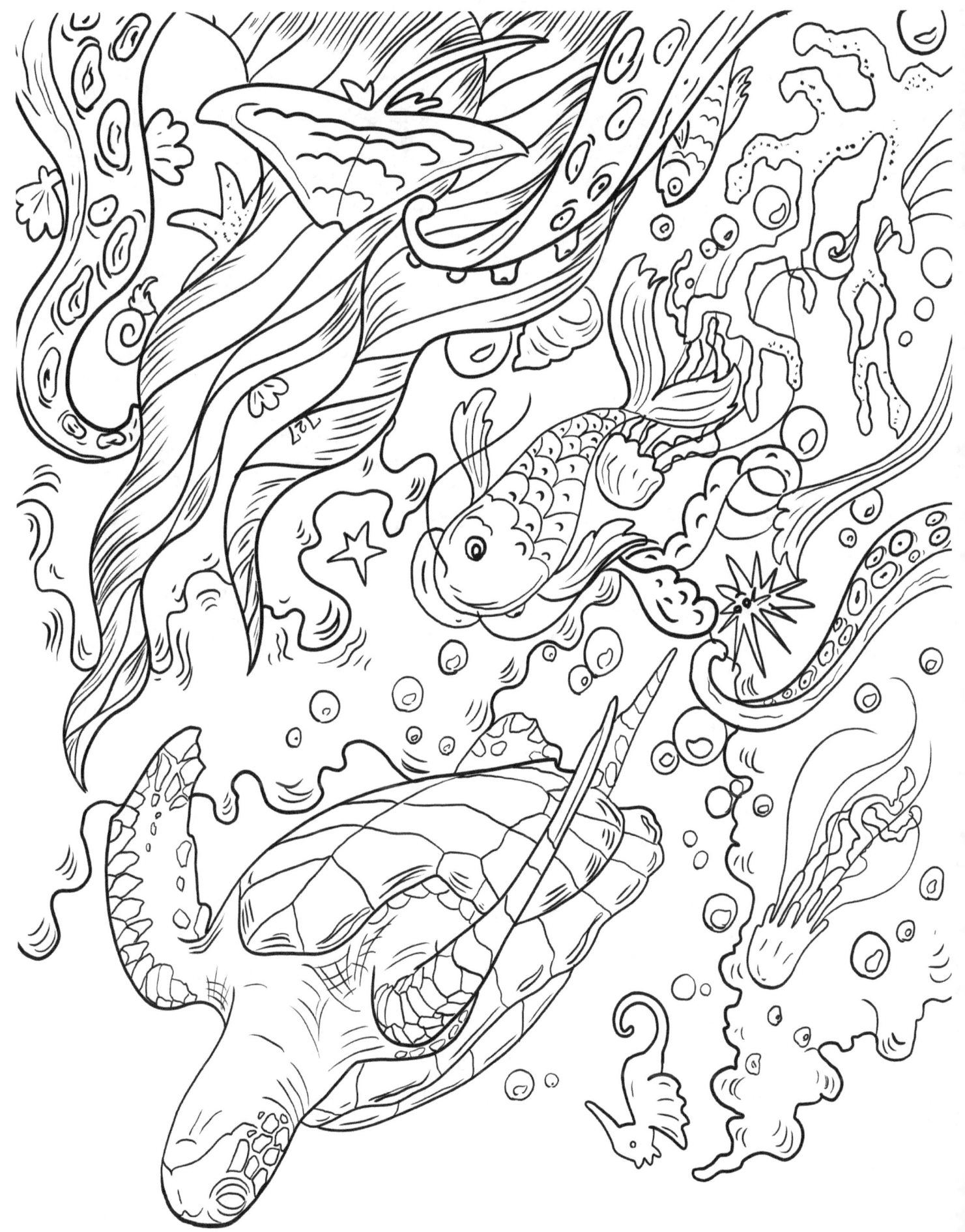

Draw something inspired by your favorite artist

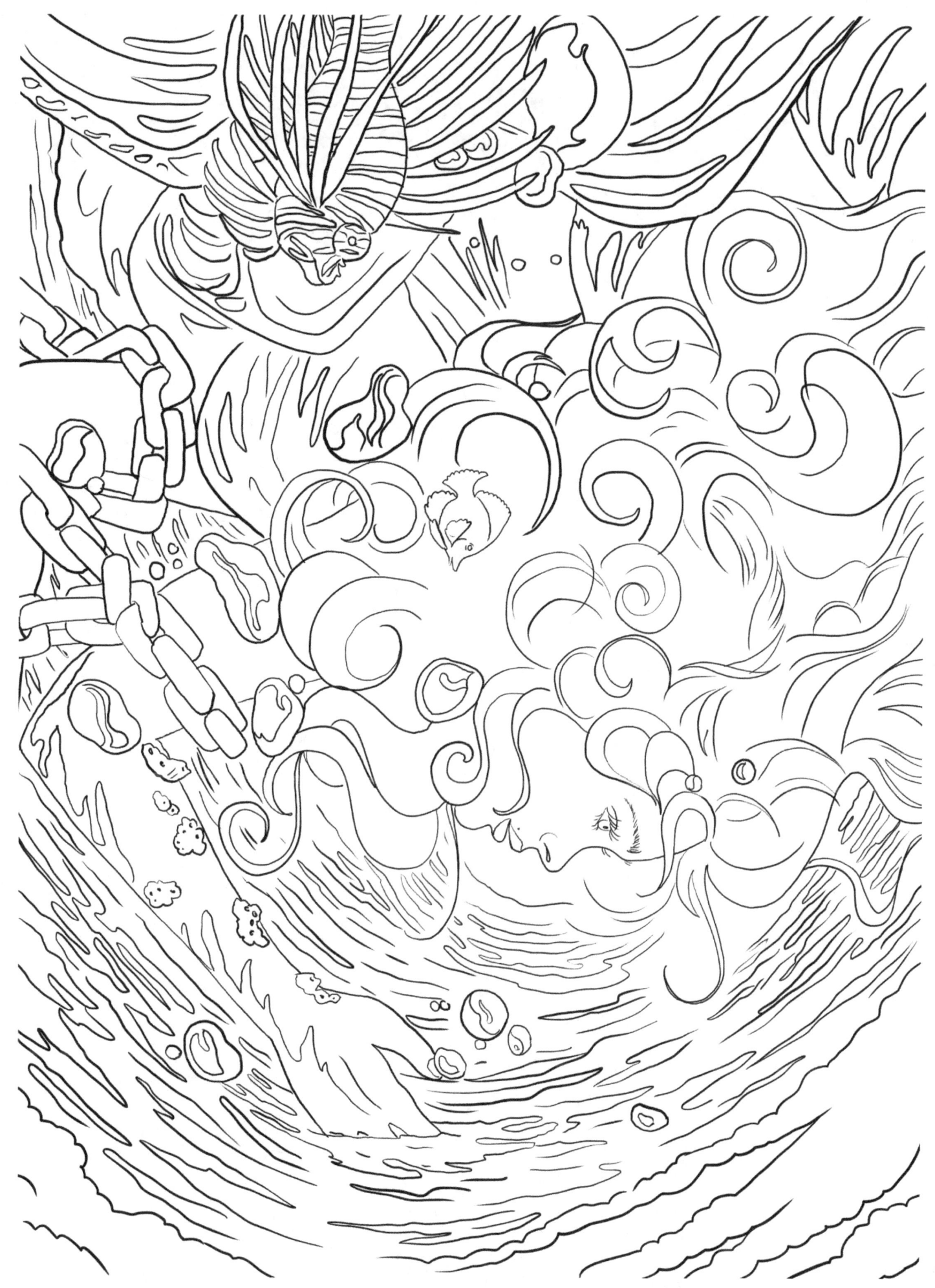

Draw something inspired by a different country

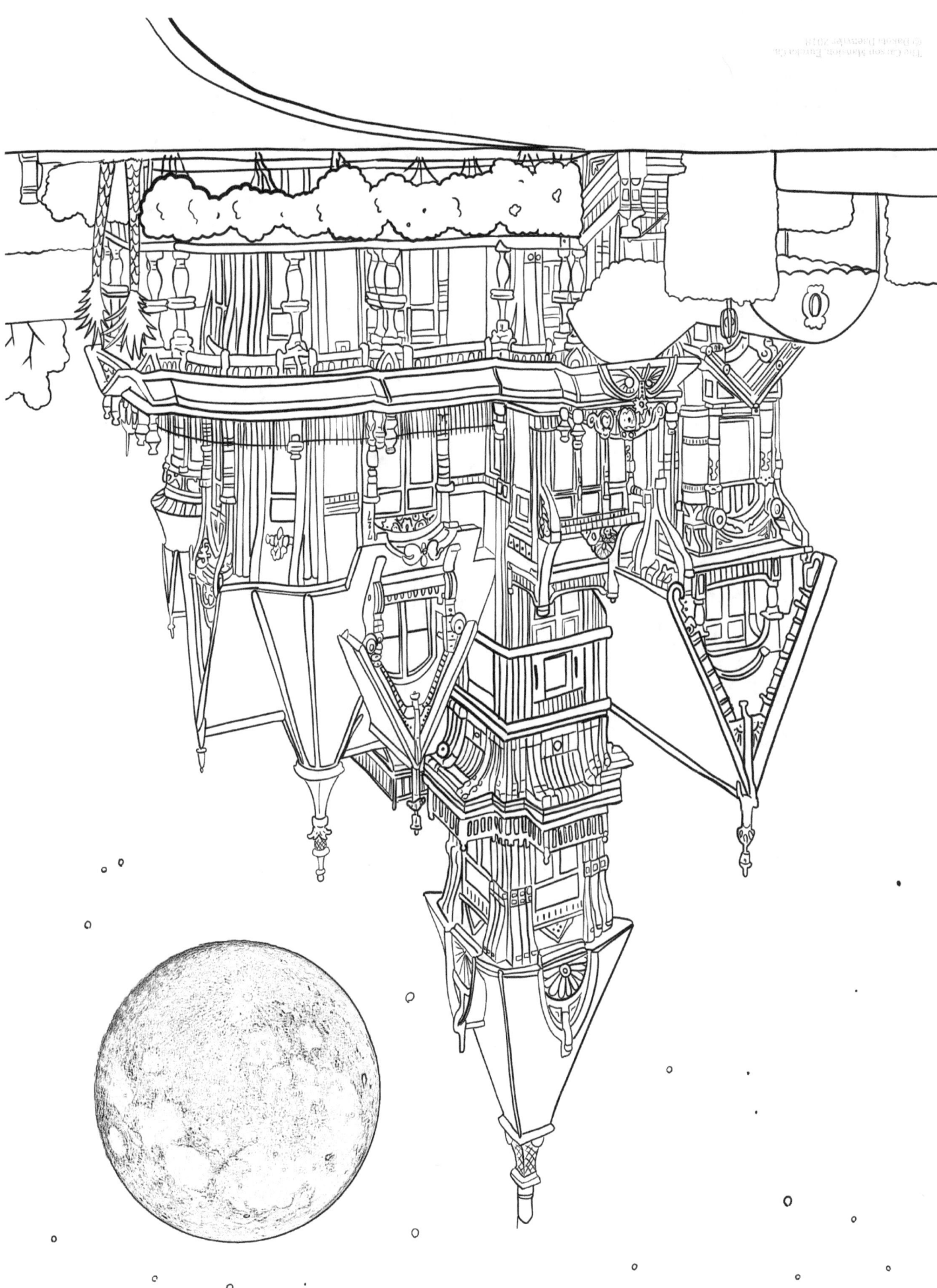

Draw your favorite local landmark

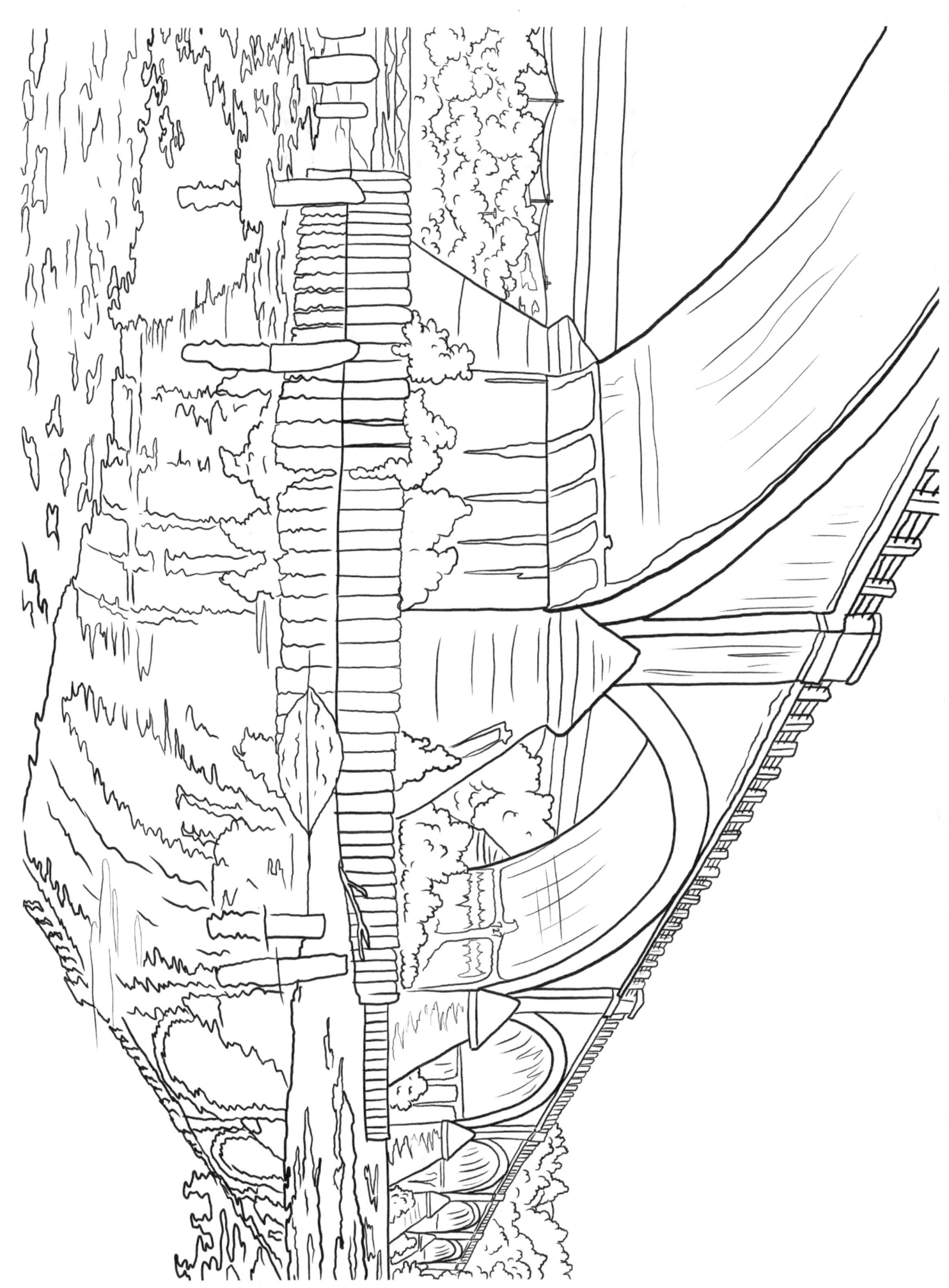

Draw Big Foot!

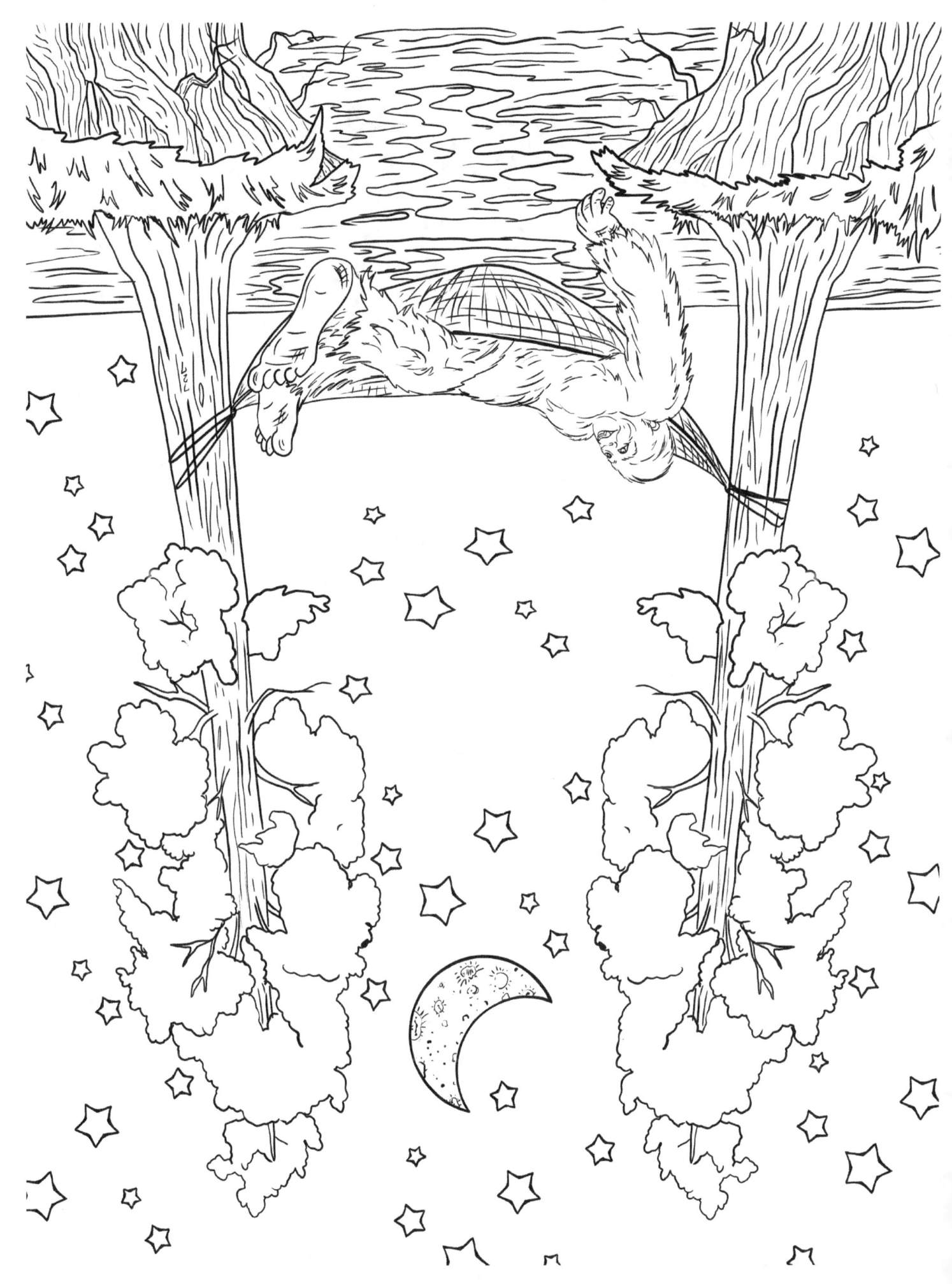

Draw some underwater creatures

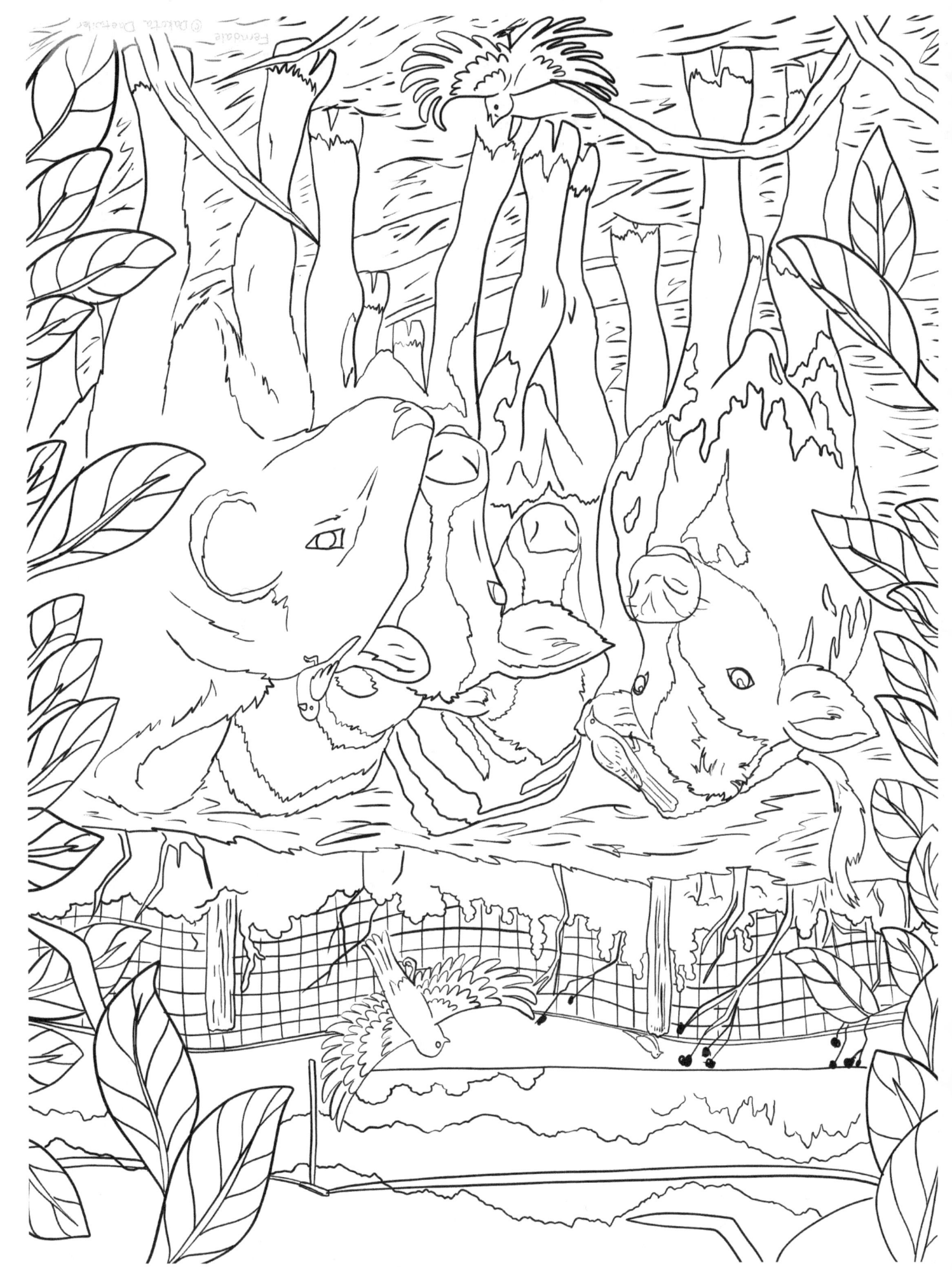

Draw a butterfly

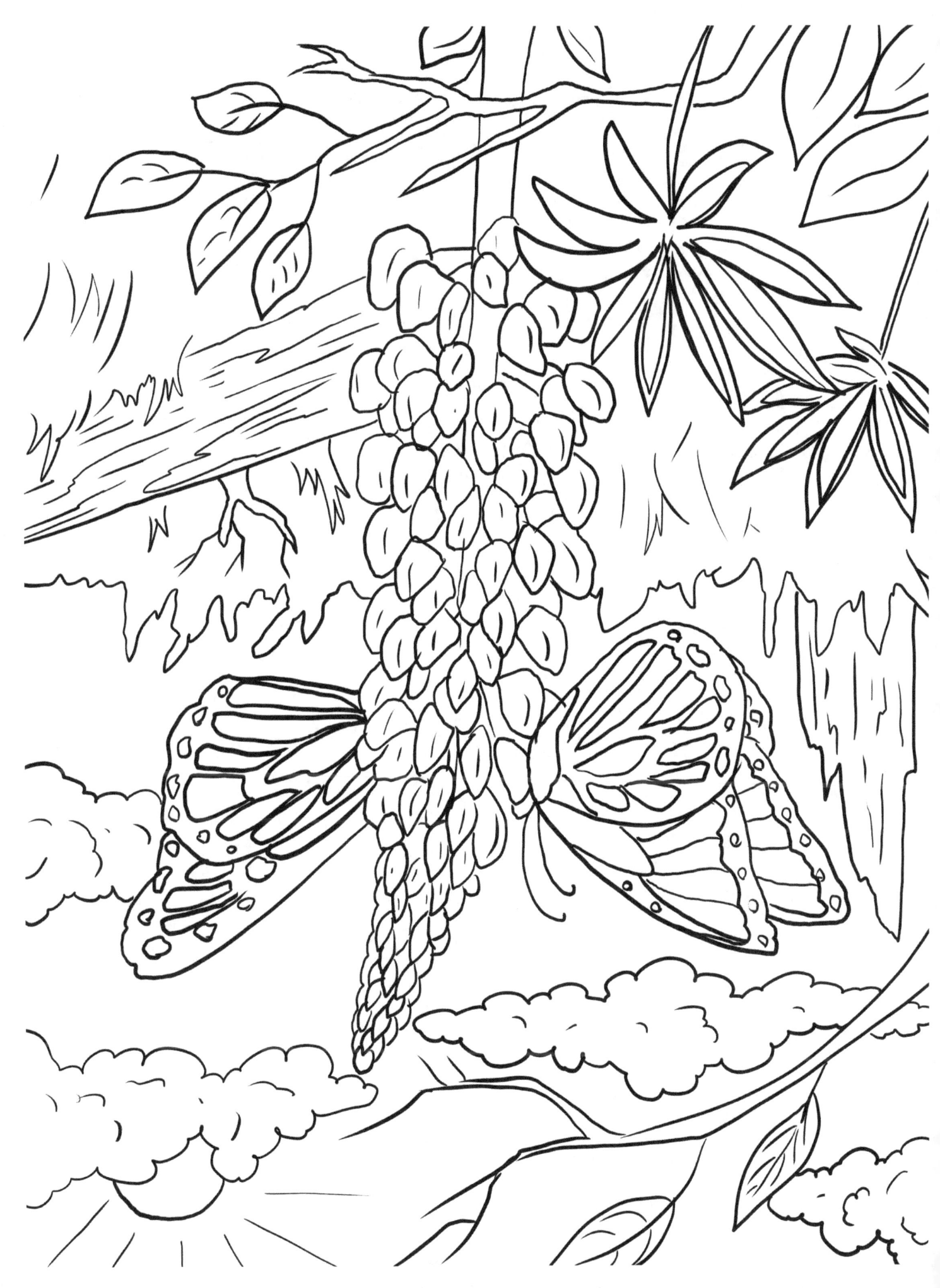

Draw an otter

Draw an otter jumping into the water

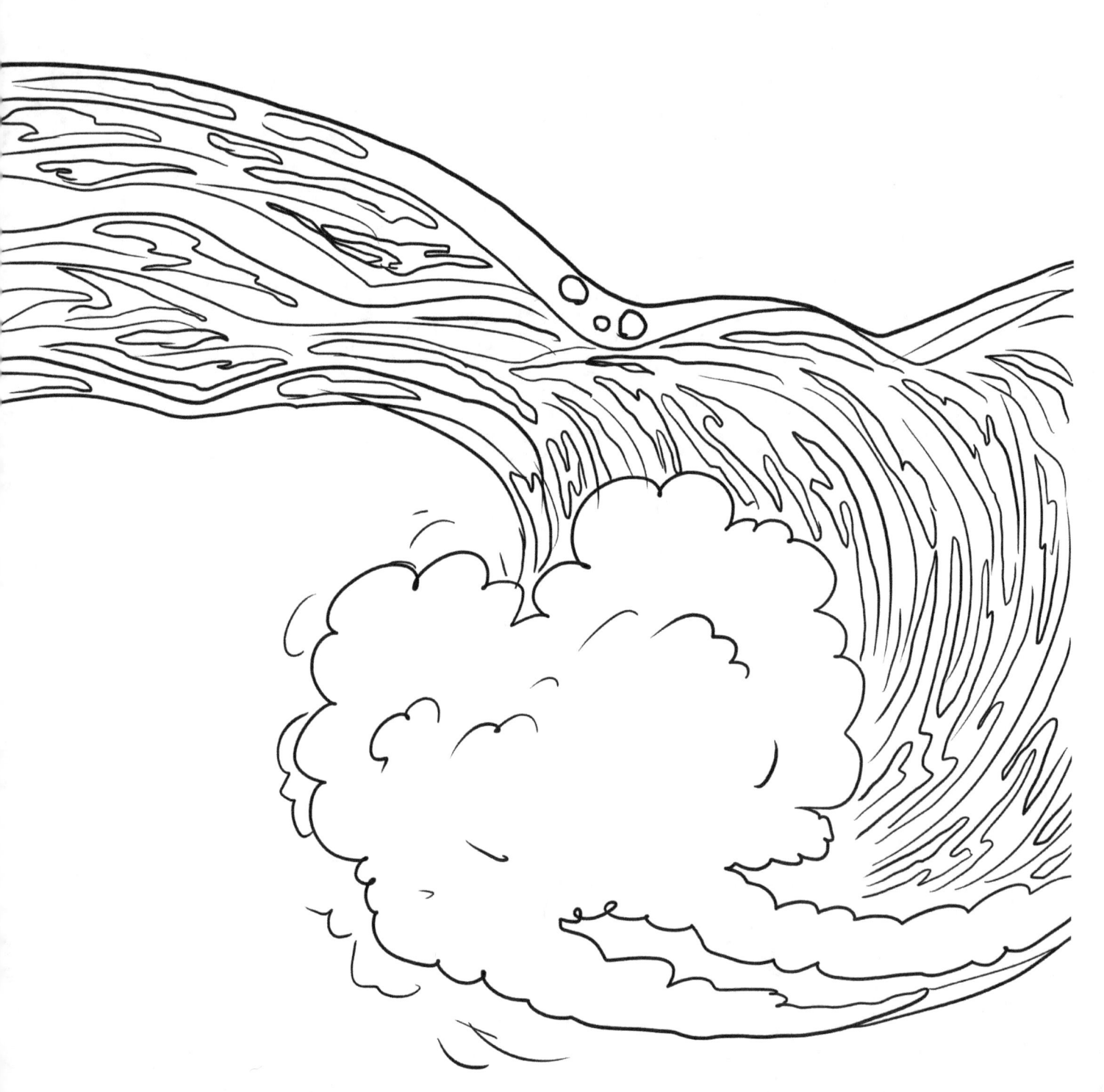

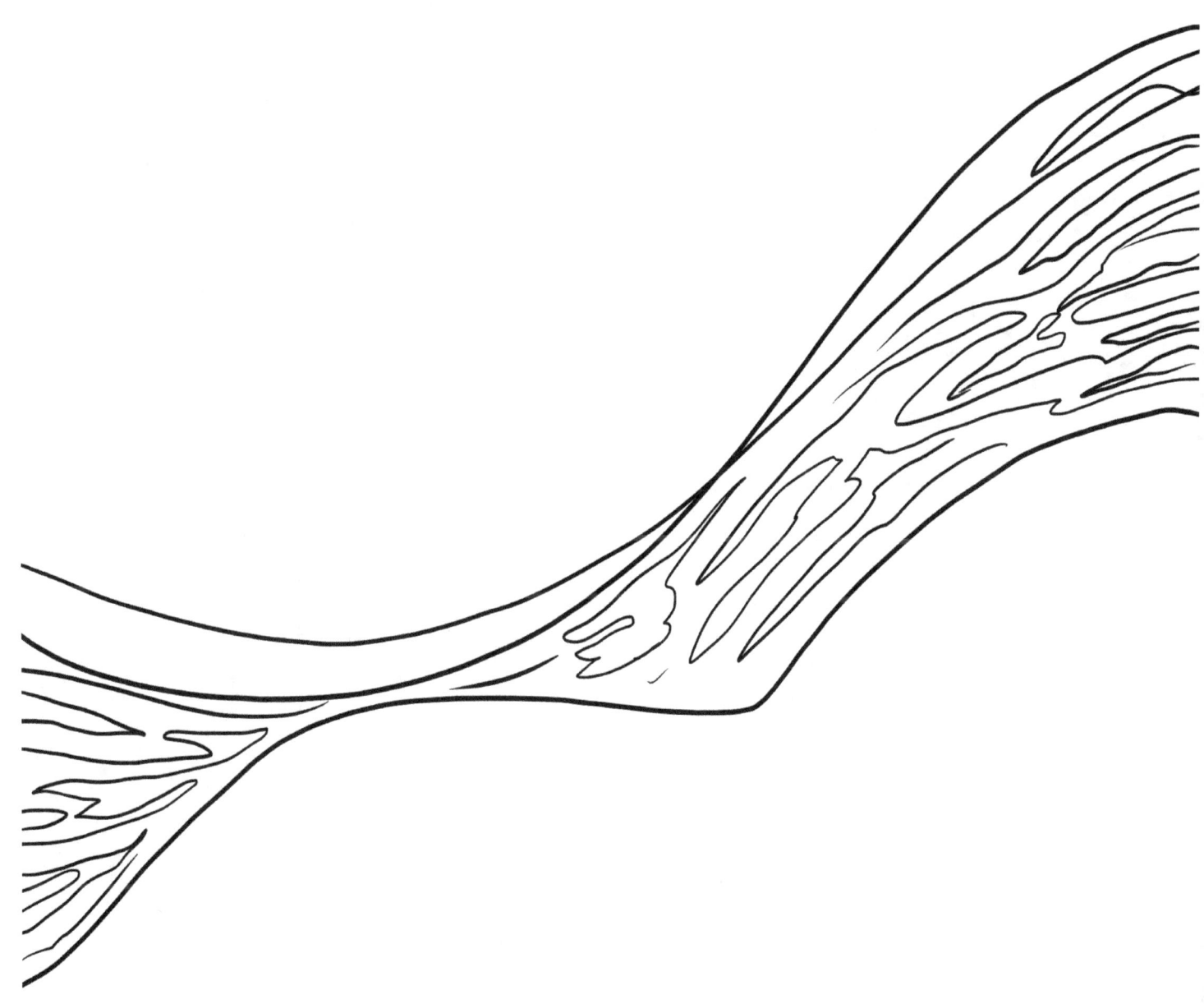

Draw and color in an underwater scene

Sketch some expressive eyes

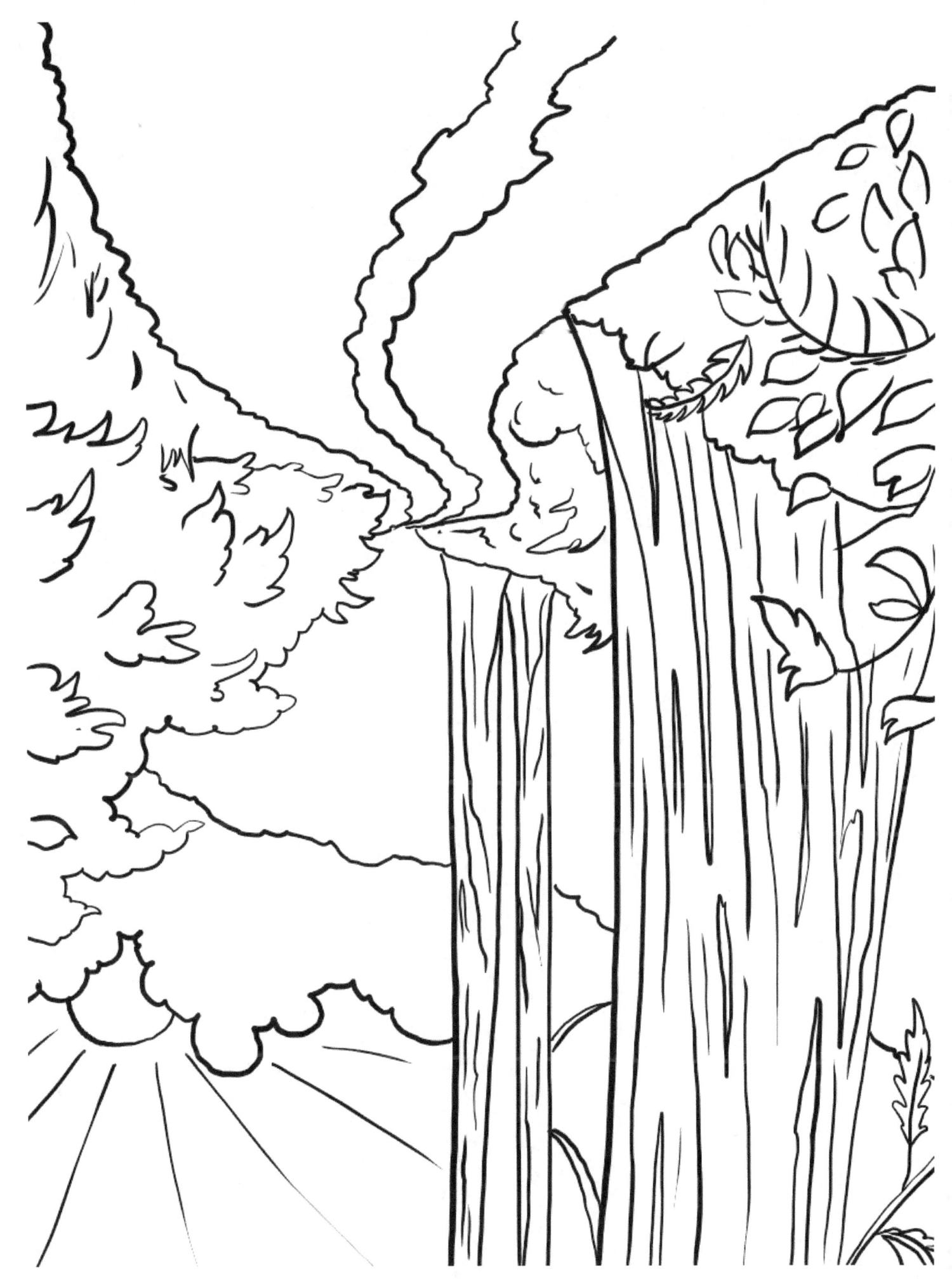

Draw a mama bear and her cubs

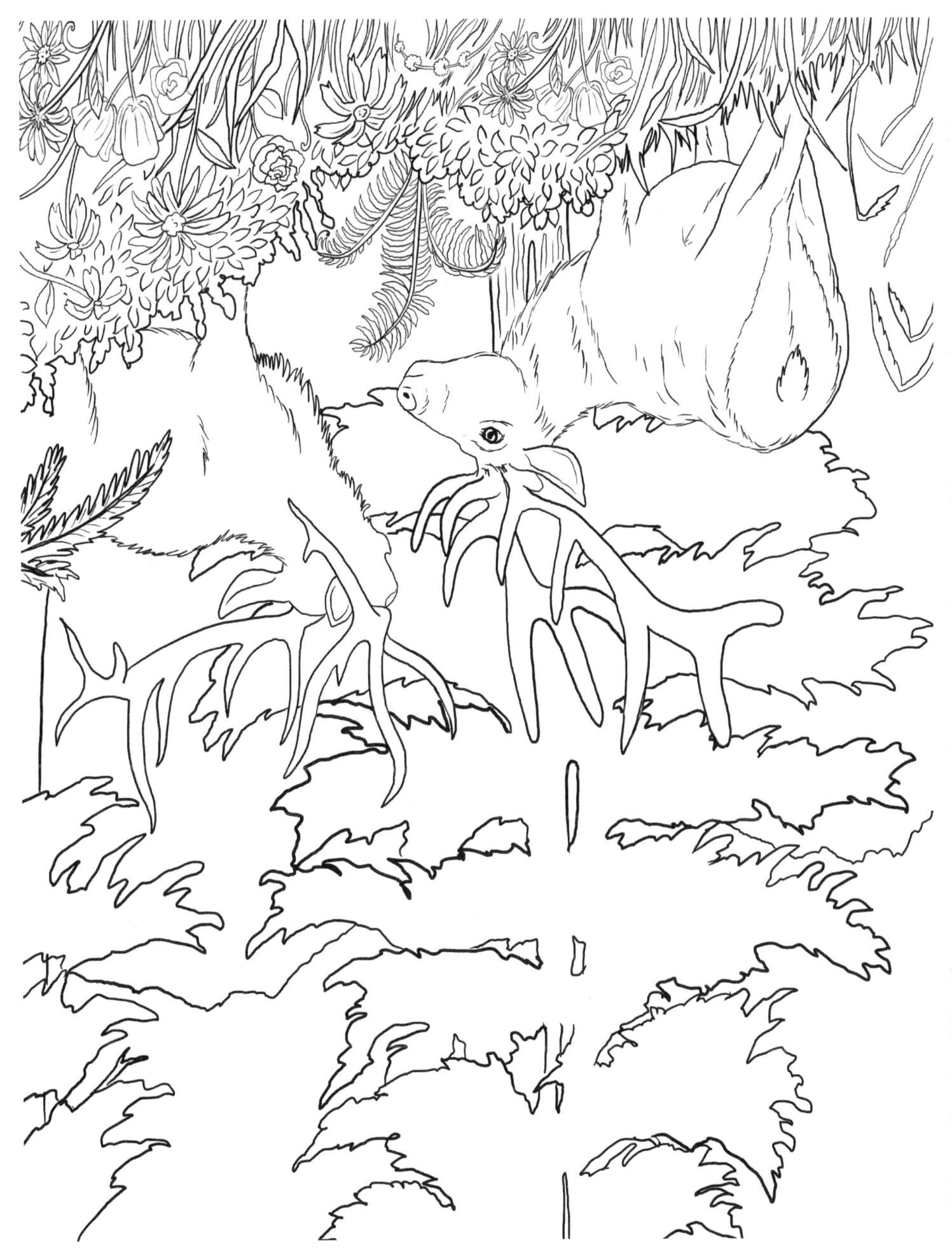

Draw an eagle flying in the sky

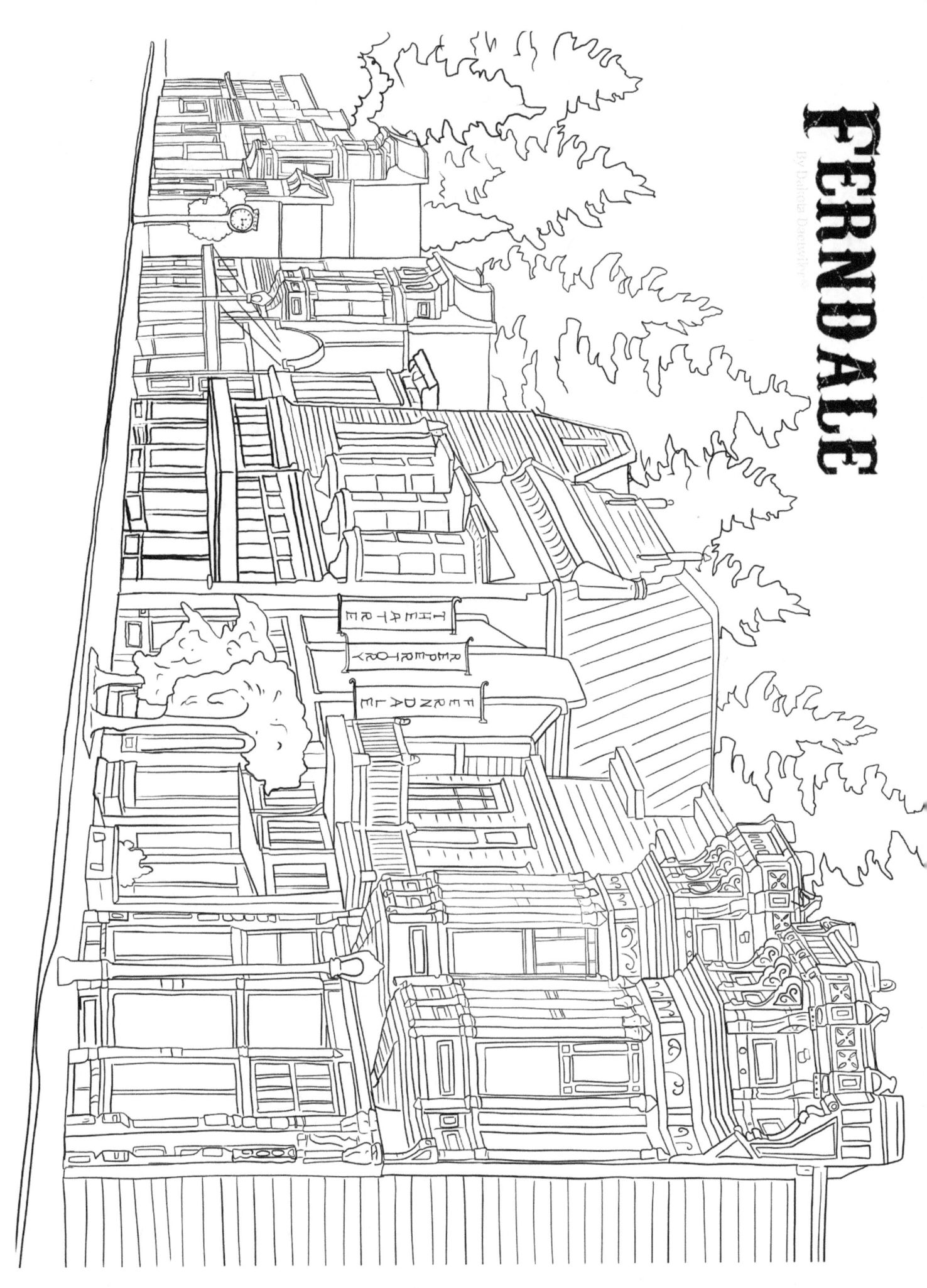

FERNDALE

By Dakota Doerwins

Draw a beach with some shells and wildlife

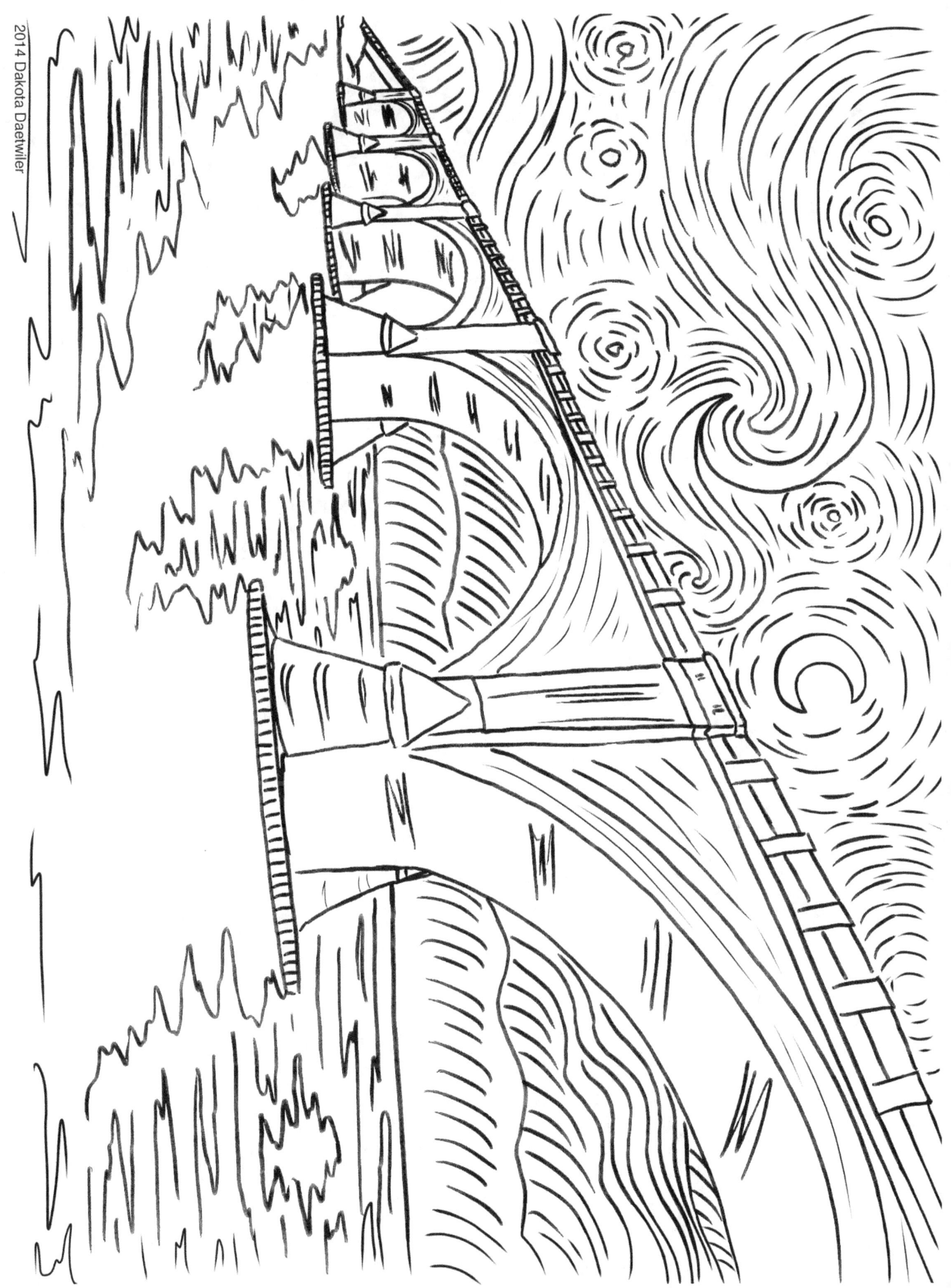

Draw a mermaid

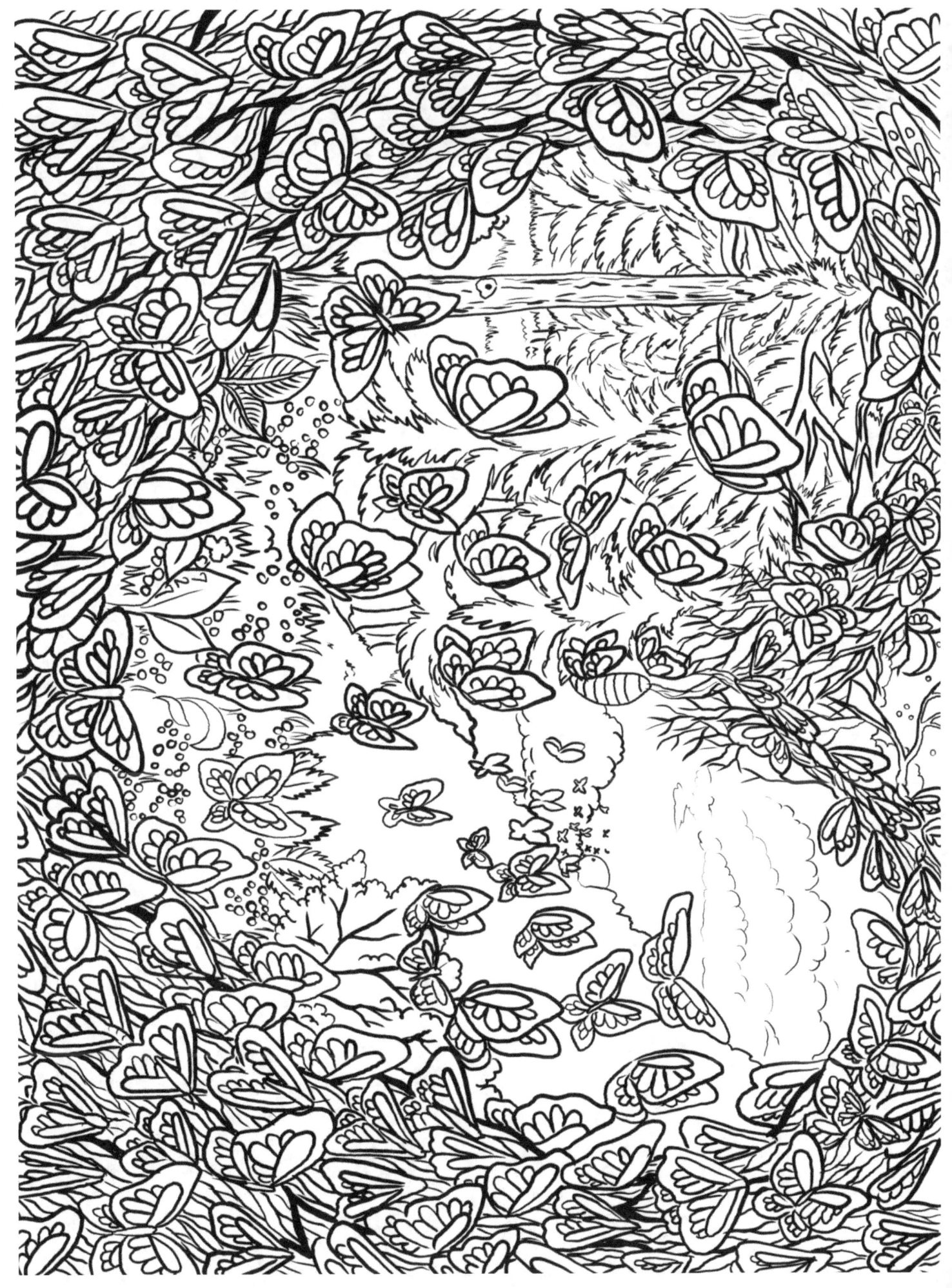

Draw a tree with snow on it

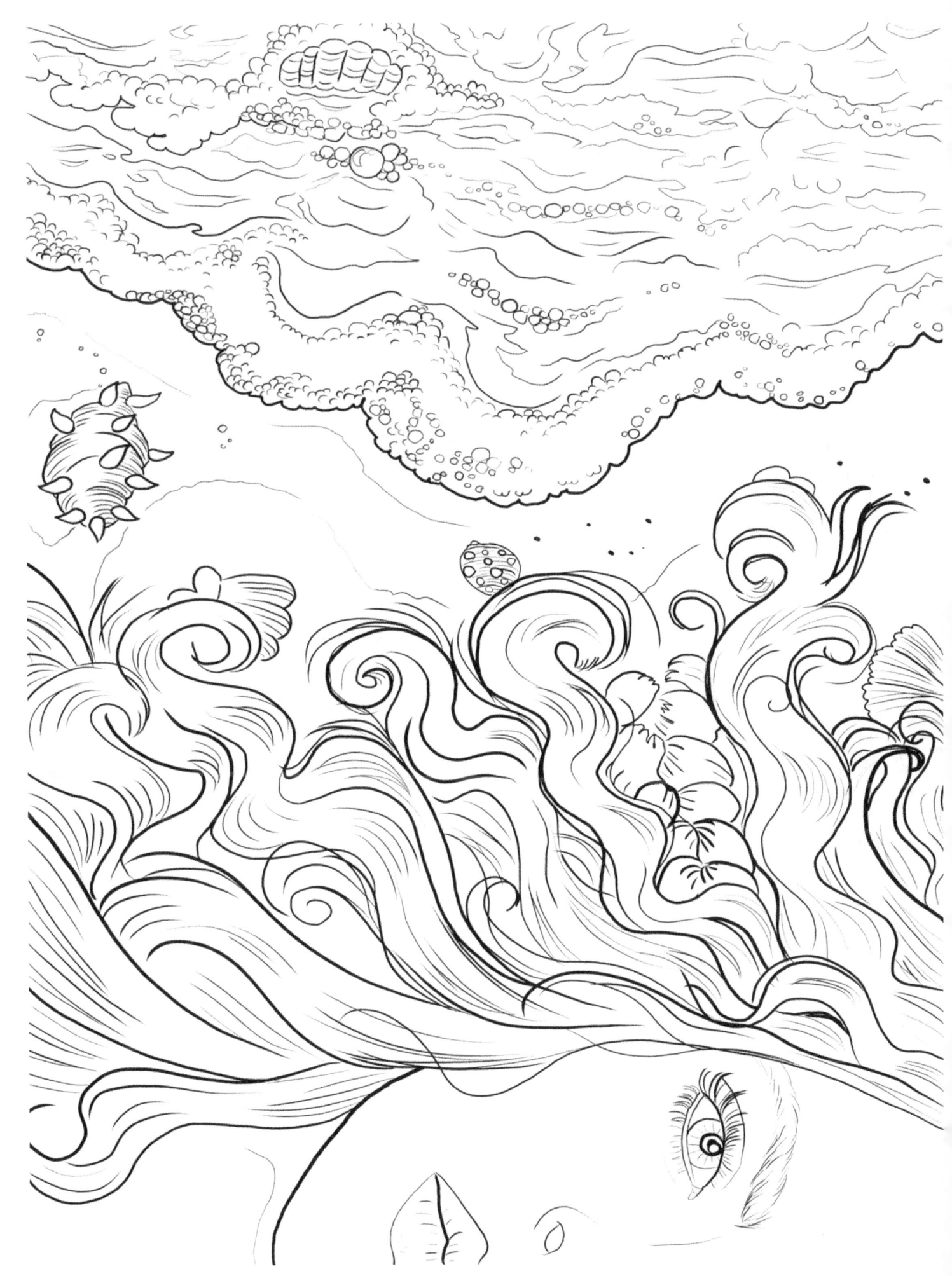

Draw your dream house

Draw your favorite pet

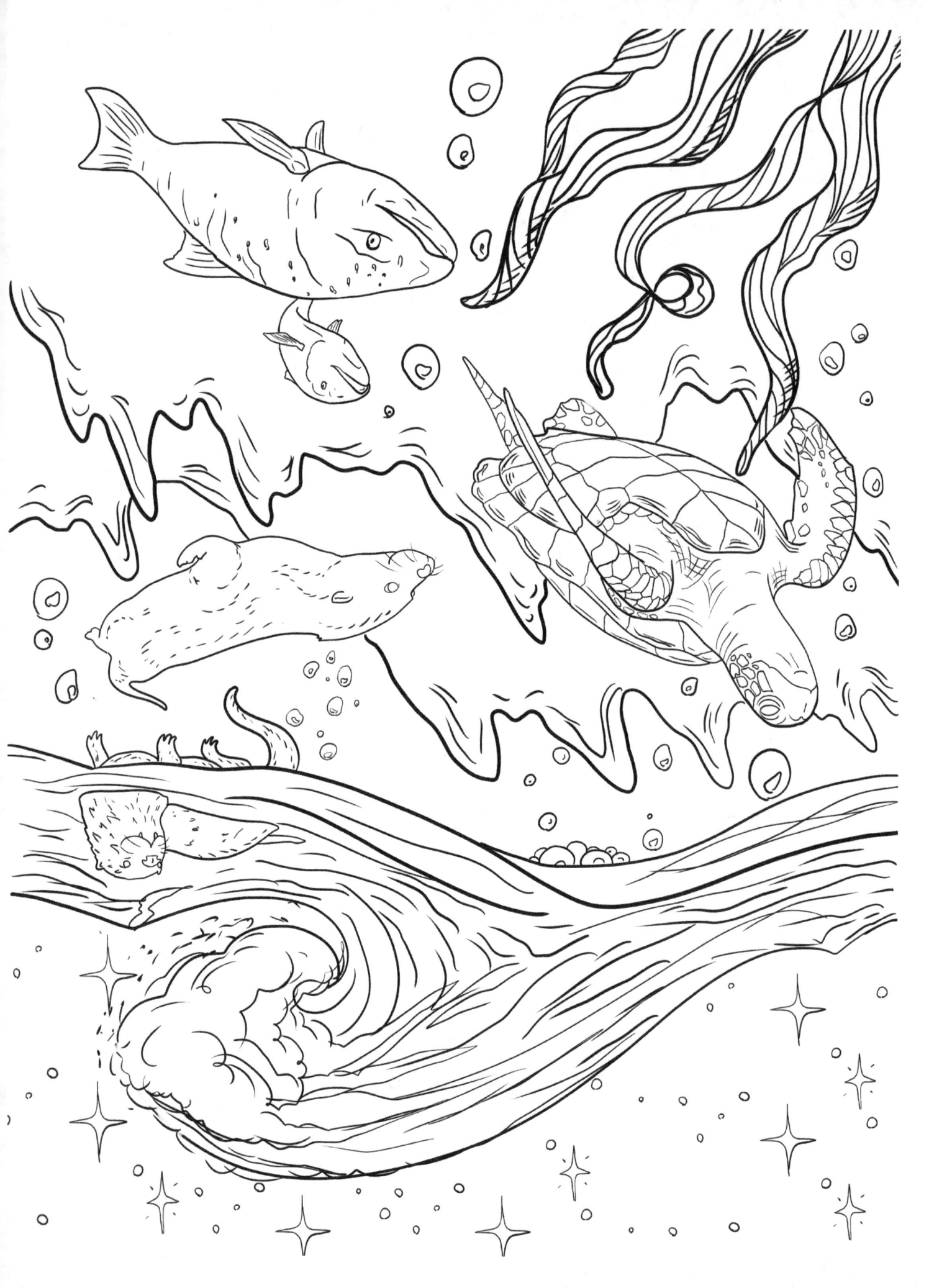

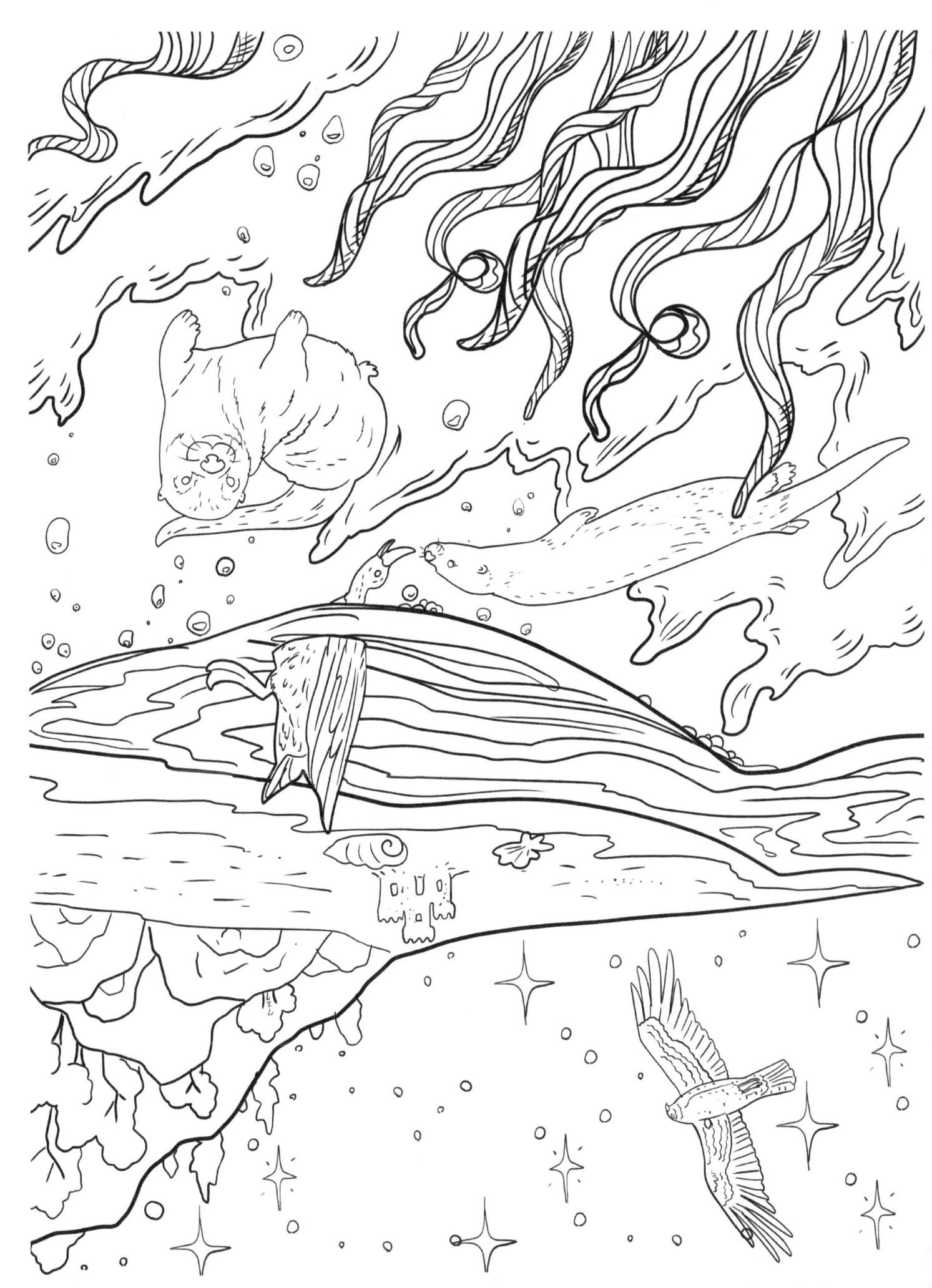

Draw your dream car

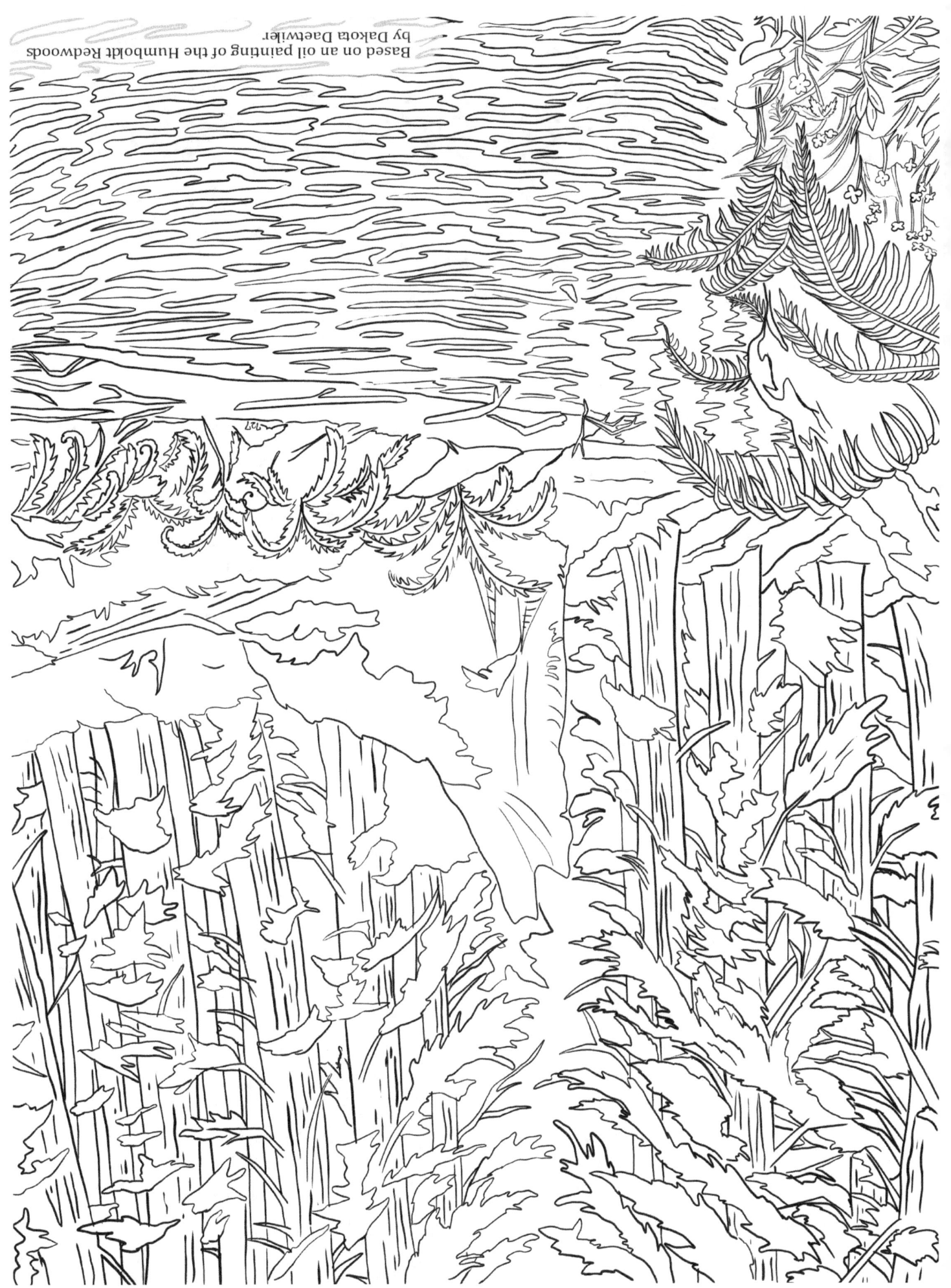

Draw a scene from a dream you've had

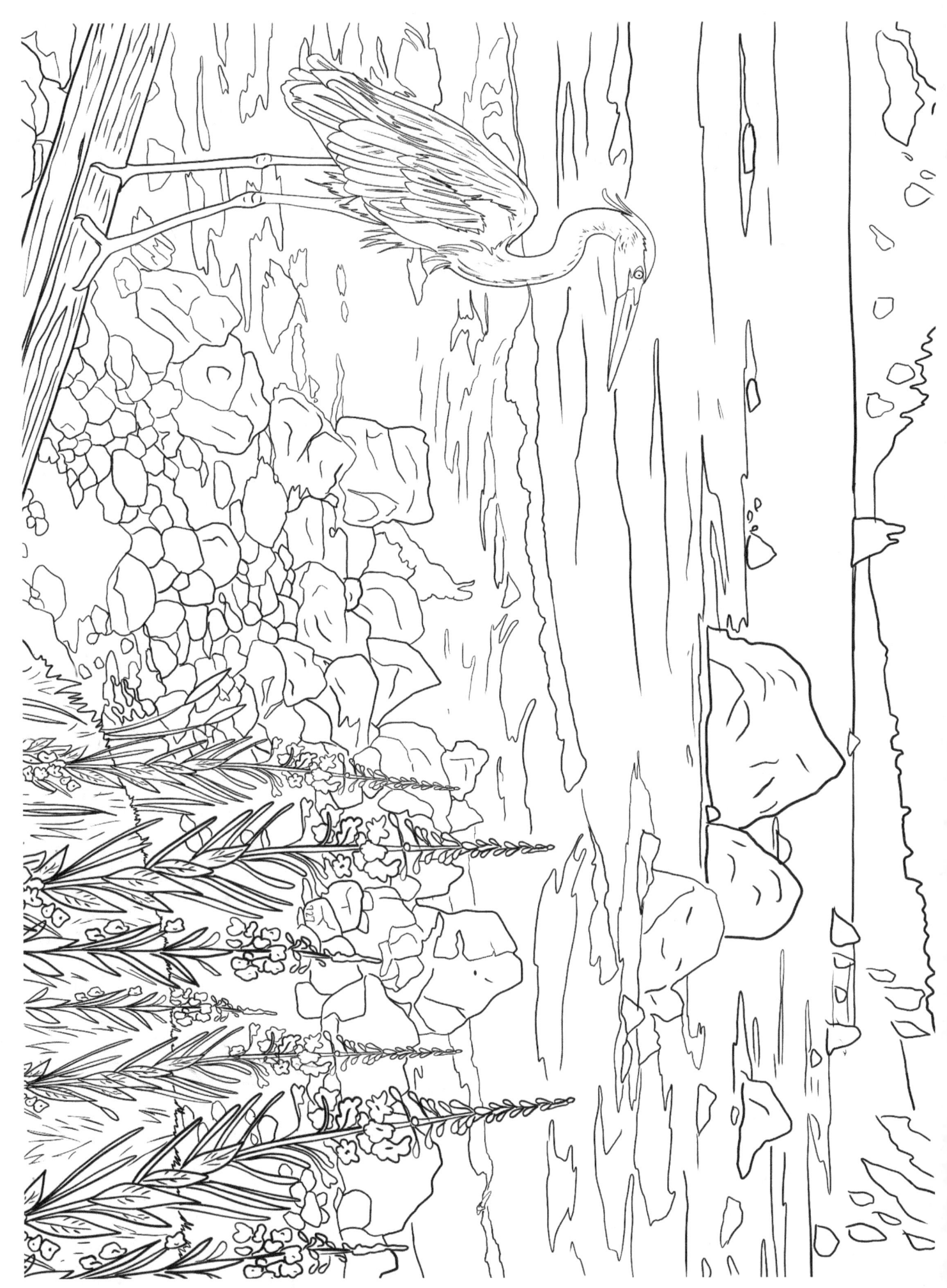

Draw your favorite character

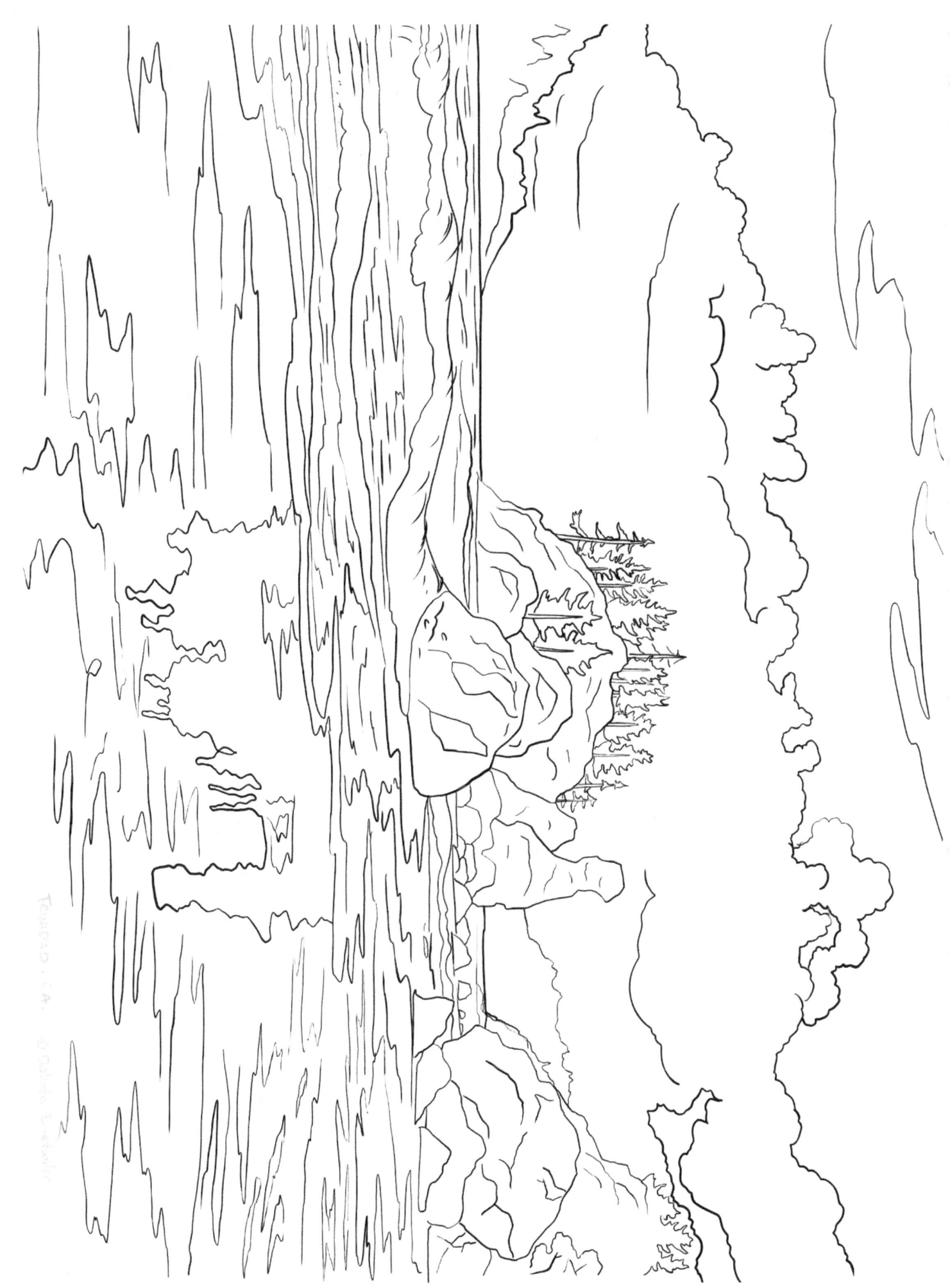

Draw your parents or siblings

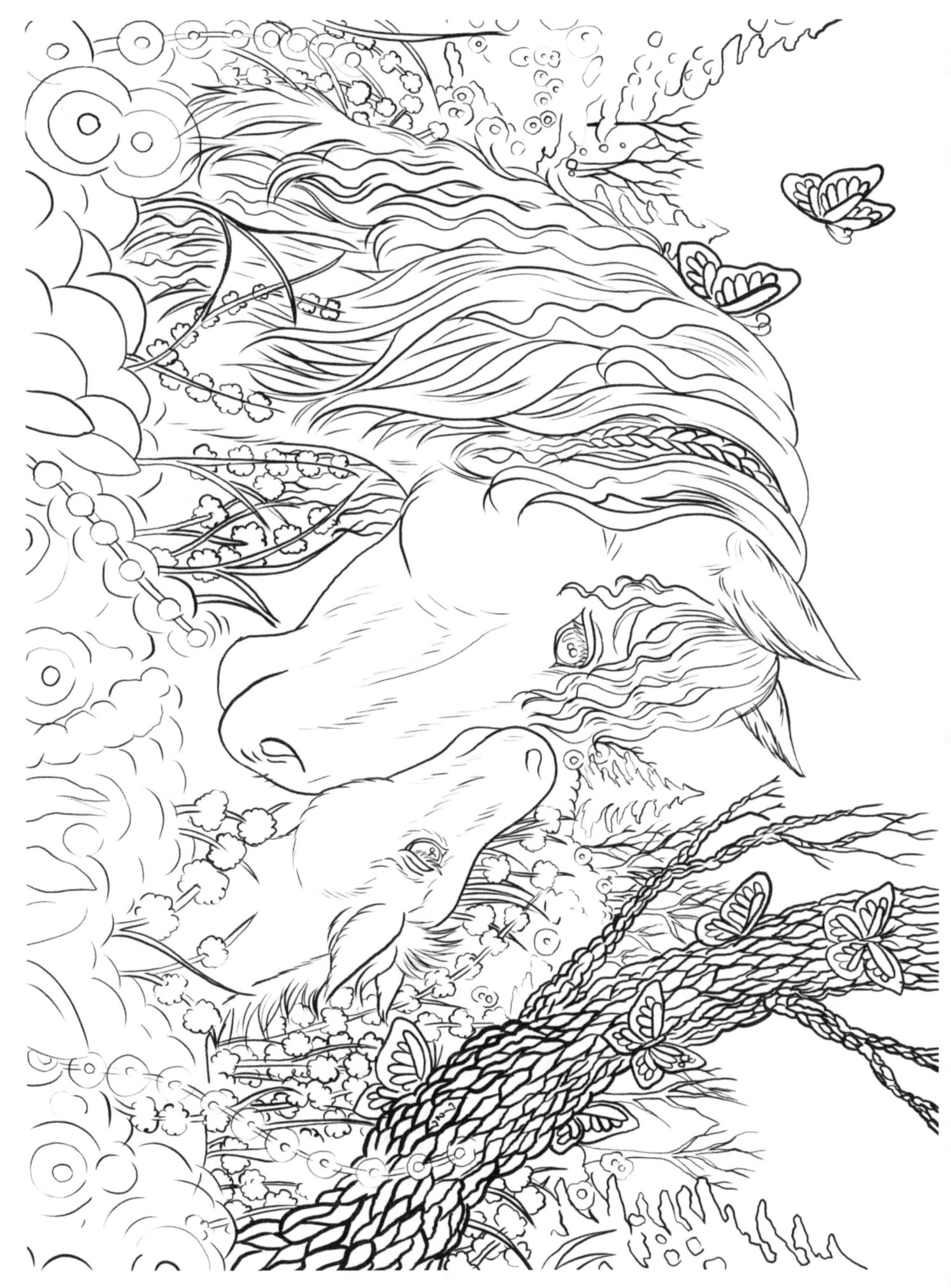

Draw your best friend

Draw an outer space scene

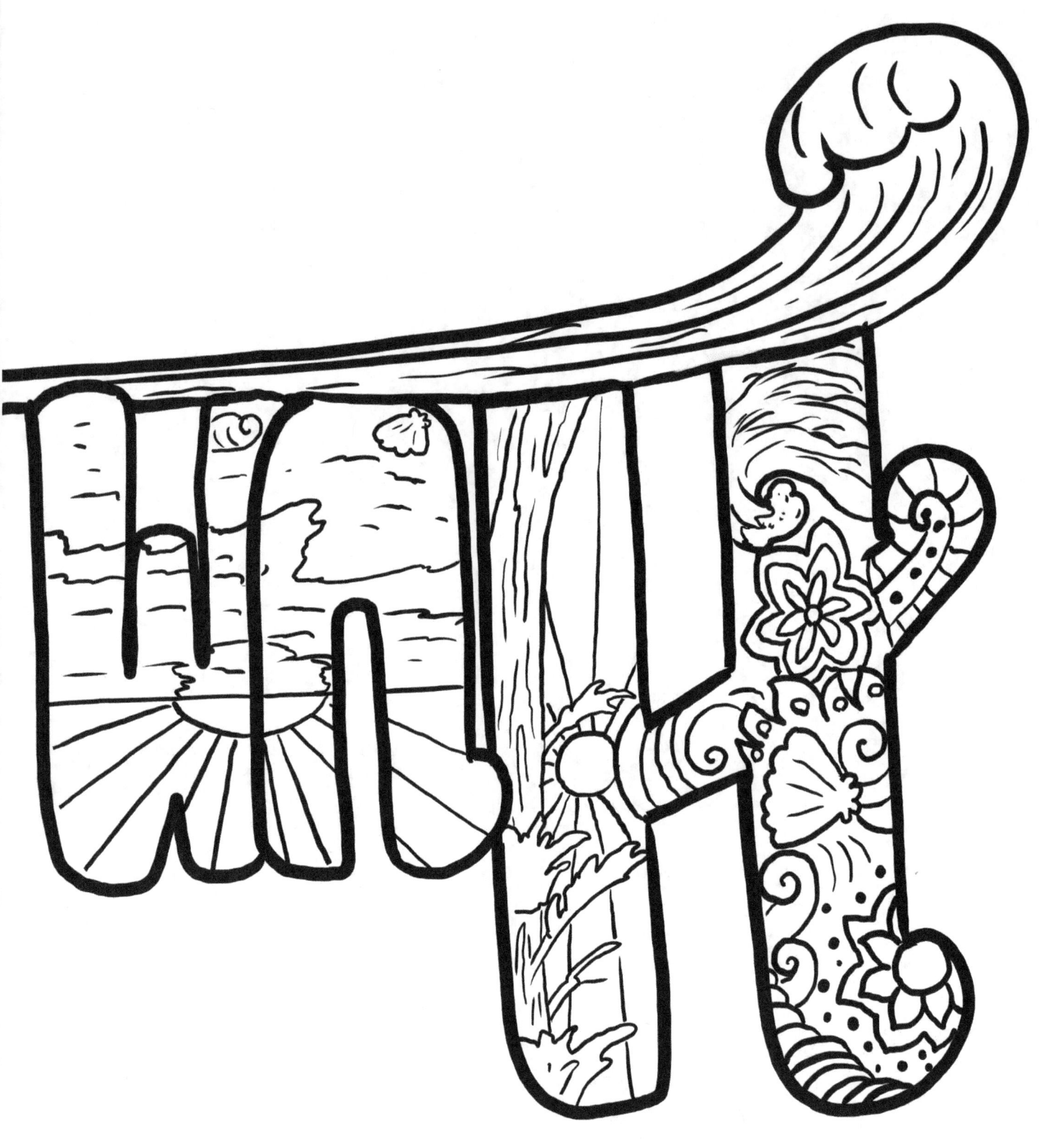

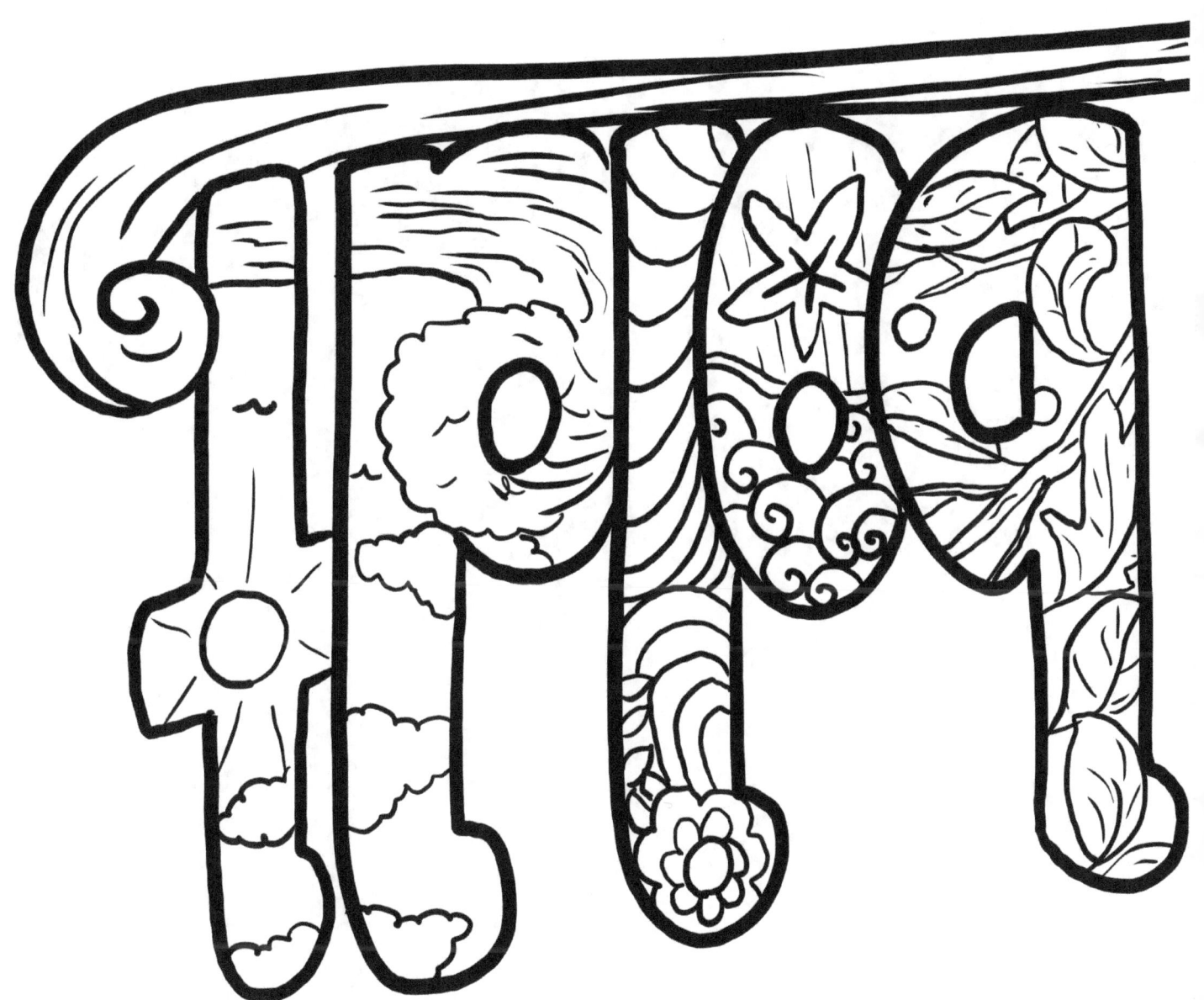

Draw your favorite thing to do in Humboldt

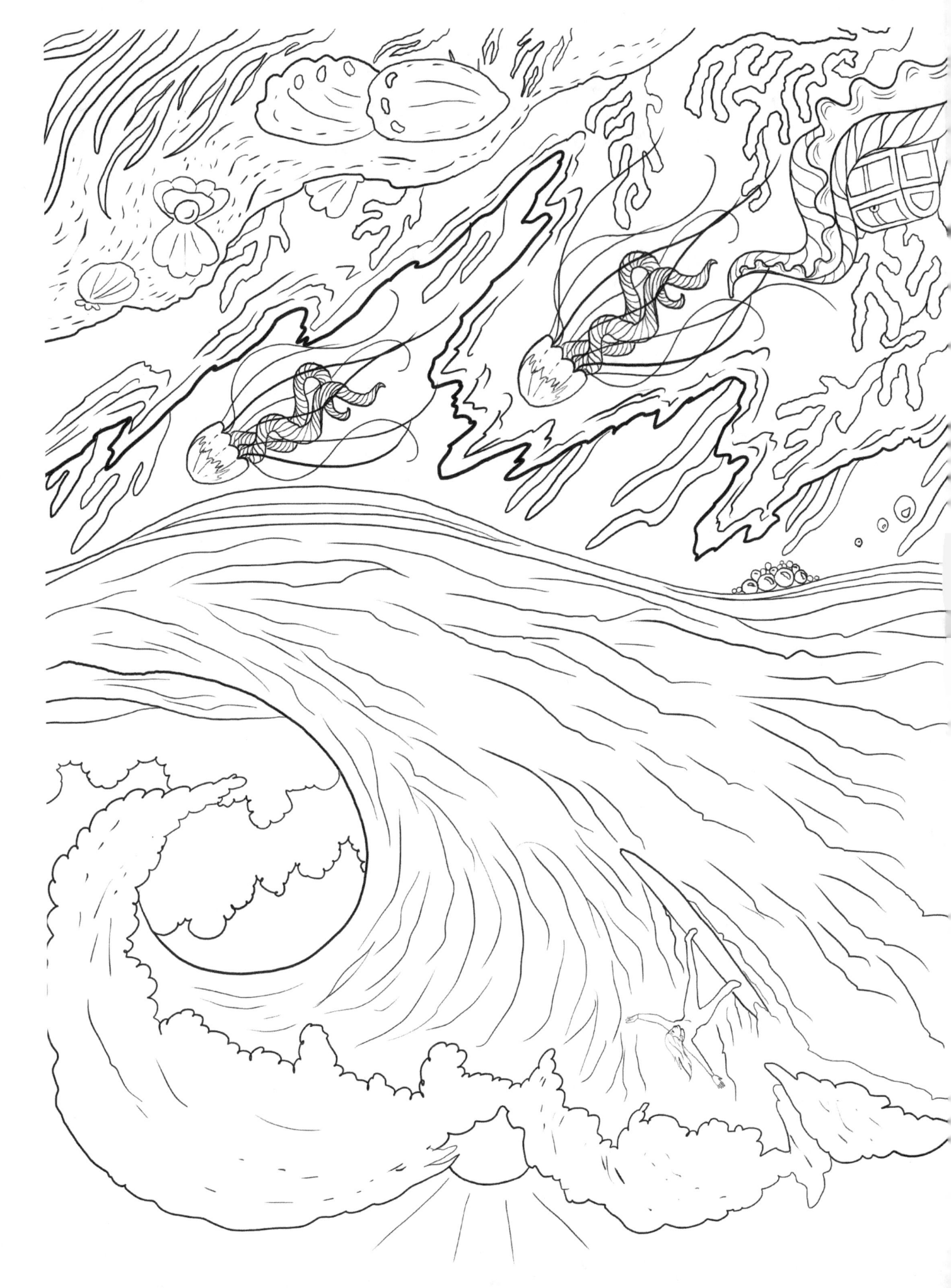

Draw what you want to be when you grow up

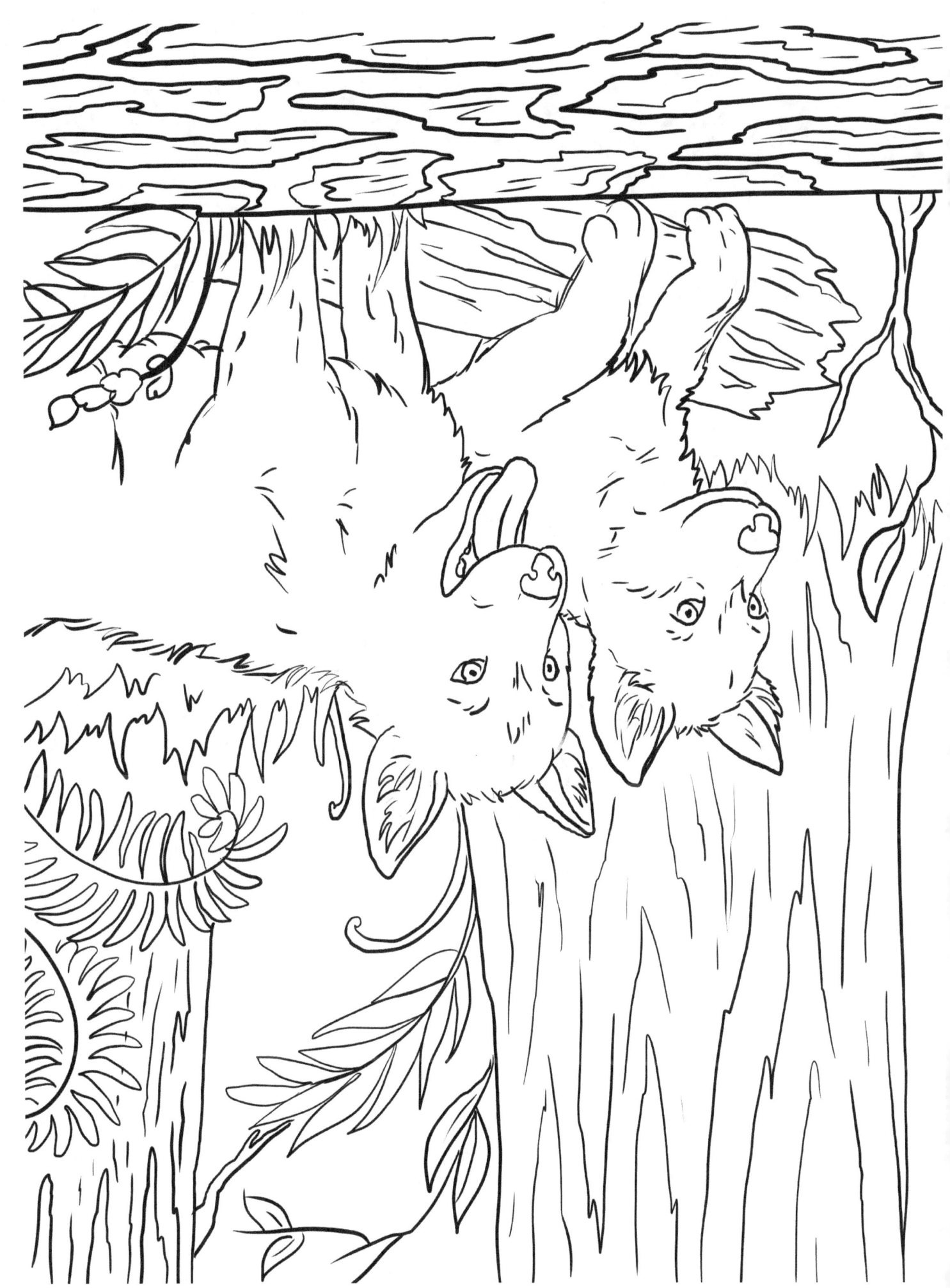